The Industrial Revolution

A History from Beginning to End

Copyright © 2019 by Hourly History.

All rights reserved.

Table of Contents

Introduction
Transport and the Rise of Global Trade
The Iron Heart of the Industrial Revolution
The Power of Steam
Mechanization of the Textile Industry
The Lives of Workers during the Industrial Revolution
The Rise of Labor Movements
Conclusion

Introduction

Revolutions that occurred between the eighteenth and twentieth centuries changed the world in a massive way. The American Revolution which ended in 1783 led to the creation of the United States as an independent country. The French Revolution which followed in 1789 changed the face of Europe and led to the rise to power of Napoleon Bonaparte. The Russian Revolution in the early years of the twentieth century involved the creation of the first Communist state and led to the emergence of the Soviet Union as a global superpower. These cataclysmic events developed quickly and led to major changes.

However, from around the middle of the eighteenth century to the middle of the nineteenth (historians still disagree about the precise dates) there was another revolution which proceeded much more slowly and less dramatically but which changed human society more profoundly than any other event during the last five hundred years. This was the Industrial Revolution, a period of rapid technological and societal change that began in Great Britain. It affected Great Britain in particular and more than any other country, but it also spread to most of the developed nations of the world. By the middle of the nineteenth century, the Industrial Revolution had directly affected virtually every person living in Europe and North America and many, many more beyond.

But just what was the Industrial Revolution? What caused it to begin, what changes did it bring, and how did it change the world so profoundly? This book looks at all these questions and aims to present the complete story of the revolution that ushered in the modern age.

Chapter One

Transport and the Rise of Global Trade

"The subject of transport is undoubtedly one of the most important questions of the present day."

—Hubert Gordon Thompson, The Canal System of England

The distance by road from London, the capital of England, to Edinburgh, the capital of Scotland, is less than four hundred miles. In the mid-eighteenth century, Great Britain was one of the most advanced countries in the world with infrastructure that was as good as that found in any other European country. Yet it took two weeks or more to travel between Edinburgh and London in a grueling journey involving heavy coaches riding on muddy, rutted roads. Few people were willing to undertake such a journey unless it was absolutely necessary, and there was no realistic possibility of sending goods produced in one city to sell them in the other. For that reason, trade was generally restricted to selling produce and goods in immediately adjacent areas. Most production centers were very small because of the problems of transporting raw materials to them and distributing finished products.

However, from around 1750, improvements in the road system in Great Britain were rapid. In the early part of the eighteenth century, most roads in England were maintained by people living in a parish who were required to work for six days every year on road maintenance. This was adequate for small, rural roads, but it left main routes in terrible condition, which accounted for the long travel time between major destinations. In the second half of the eighteenth century, large numbers of local authorities applied for turnpike trusts, acts of parliament which allowed them to build new roads and to charge a toll to traffic using these roads to recoup the costs. Turnpike trusts, combined with advances in road building technology pioneered by engineers such as Thomas Telford and John McAdam, led to a dramatic improvement in the quality of British roads—by the early 1800s, the travel time between London and Edinburgh had been reduced to two days rather than two weeks.

Although the improvements in the roads led to rapid reduction in the time taken for passengers to travel between British cities, there was still a major problem with the movement of heavy bulk goods. Transporting these by using horse-drawn road vehicles was slow and expensive. This was particularly true for coal. The demand for coal in Britain was high during the eighteenth century, both from manufacturing and for private use—there had been a national shortage of wood in Britain from the end of the seventeenth century, and coal was the main form of heating for virtually every British household in the mid-1700s. Coal mines were often far distant from centers of population, and the primary means of transport was by ships using rivers or the sea. This left the supply of coal at the mercy of weather and tides and kept prices high. It also made it very difficult for mines which were not close to ports to be commercially viable.

As with so many of the developments which propelled the Industrial Revolution, the solution to the transport of heavy bulk goods within Britain was solved by a single, far-sighted, and bold entrepreneur. Francis Egerton, the third duke of Bridgewater, was just 23 years old and owned a complex of coal mines near the town of Worsley in Lancashire. The mines supplied the local area with coal, but transport to the city of Manchester, forty miles away, was slow and expensive. The horse-drawn carts in use at the time could hold only up to three tons of coal and took two or three days to make the journey. This meant that coal was very expensive in Manchester—the mines at Worsley were the closest coal mines to the city. In 1759, Egerton decided that he would have a canal built, linking his mines with the city.

It was a bold and difficult project. All previous canals in Britain (and there were few at the time) had followed the course of existing rivers. The duke proposed something completely new—a canal which did not follow the route of any watercourse and would require the construction of viaducts and cuttings to reach Manchester. Many people were skeptical about whether this was possible or could be commercially viable; nevertheless Egerton was able to obtain an Act of Parliament which made construction possible. Work began in late 1759, and the canal opened in July 1761. Egerton invested over £168,000 of his own money to build the canal (worth over £23 million today) which included several miles of underground canal serving several of his coal mines.

The canal was used by large barges, each capable of carrying thirty tons of coal. A single horse walking on the towpath was capable of towing one barge. This made the bulk transport of coal much more economical, and within weeks of the canal opening, the price of coal in Manchester had dropped by more than 50%, making the mines at Worsley very profitable indeed. Other people took note of the success of the canal, and by 1770, Britain had entered what would become known as the period of Canal Mania. A network of canals was built connecting the cities of the Midlands with Lancashire and Yorkshire and the emerging industrial areas of Staffordshire. The canal system was later extended as far south as London, and by 1790, it was possible to transport coal by canal from the mines at Worsley to the River Thames at Oxford. By the early nineteenth century, Britain was served by a network of over four thousand miles of canals.

The canals enabled the transport of all kinds of raw materials and manufactured goods—the famous manufacturer of pottery, Josiah Wedgwood, used canals to bring clay to his potteries in Staffordshire and to safely export the finished pottery, minimizing the chance of breakage and waste. The canal system changed the transport of bulk cargoes within Great Britain beyond recognition within the space of little more than fifty years.

It wasn't only transport within Britain that was significant during this period. In the mid-1700s, Great Britain had extensive colonies in North America, Africa, and Asia. Other European countries, including France, Spain, Portugal, and the Netherlands, also had colonies around the world. Sailing ships brought raw materials from the colonies to Europe and manufactured goods from Europe to the colonies. Great Britain, in particular, was involved in what became called the triangular trade. British merchant ships would buy sugar (or molasses, the liquid form of sugar) in the Caribbean. The sugar would then be taken either back to Britain or to British colonies in New England where it was sold for distillation into rum. The profits from the sale of sugar or molasses were used to buy manufactured goods in the local area. These were then taken to British colonies on the west coast of Africa where they were traded for slaves. The slaves were taken to the Caribbean where they were sold to plantation owners and the profits were used to buy sugar or molasses to start the whole route over again. It took around twelve weeks for a ship to complete one circumnavigation of this route which could be repeated several times each year. The triangular trade was immensely profitable, making many traders extremely wealthy.

There were many other trade routes which brought material from the colonies to Britain—cotton, for example, was brought from India and tobacco from the Caribbean. Britain also exported manufactured goods, particularly fabrics and metalware, to the colonies. In the 1600s, most British trade had been with nearby European countries. By the late 1700s, 57% of all British exports of manufactured goods went to America and the West Indies, and 32% of imports of raw materials came from the same sources. Improvements in the internal transport system provided by the building of canals made it much easier for exports to be rapidly, economically, and reliably moved to British ports and for imported raw materials to be transported to British manufacturing centers.

Improvements in the transport system within Great Britain combined with increasing international trade were vital and often unrecognized drivers that helped provide the conditions which enabled the explosion of the Industrial Revolution.

Chapter Two

The Iron Heart of the Industrial Revolution

"The significant thing about the Darbys and coke-iron is not that the first Abraham Darby 'invented' a new process but that five generations of the Darby connection were able to perfect it and develop most of its applications."

—Anthony F. C. Wallace, *Essays on Culture Change*

One material was more important in the Industrial Revolution than any other: iron. Iron had been produced in Great Britain for over five thousand years. Iron ore, like coal, is found in many parts of Britain. Early ironworks were generally small-scale affairs built close to both sources of iron ore and forests which provided the charcoal needed for the reduction of the ore during the smelting process. However, even the relatively small-scale ironworks existing in Britain in the early part of the eighteenth century consumed around two hundred acres of forest each year. Wood was becoming both scarce and expensive in Great Britain in the early 1700s, just as the demand for iron was increasing and iron began to be imported from Europe.

There had been a number of attempts to produce iron using cheap coal instead of charcoal, but this was found to create iron which was brittle and unreliable. Then, in 1709, a brass worker named Abraham Darby purchased a semi-derelict blast furnace in Coalbrookdale in Shropshire. There were several coal mines nearby, and Darby set out to find a way to use coal rather than charcoal to make iron. He discovered that the problem with using coal for smelting was the production of large quantities of sulfur which produced impurities in the iron and made it brittle. However, if coal was heated in the absence of air, it turned into a hard, grey combustible material known as coke. During the process of converting coal into coke, most of the sulfur is burned off as a gas, and Darby discovered that using coke in the smelting process produced high-quality iron more cheaply than using charcoal.

The new process was so successful that Darby opened a second ironworks in 1715, and when he died in 1717, the business was taken over by his son, Abraham Darby II, who refined the production of coke by burning coal in special ovens, resulting in even higher quality iron. The Darby family retained the secret of using coke to produce high-quality iron for almost fifty years. The ironworks at Coalbrookdale became very profitable, producing everything from parts for the ship-building industry, pots and pans, and even components for the steam pumps which were beginning to be used in mines across the country. The grandson of the original innovator, Abraham Darby III, continued to refine the process of iron production and used iron from the Coalbrookdale works to build the first iron bridge in the world across the River Severn in 1779.

The success of the Darby family and their iron production was of course partly enabled by improvements in the transport infrastructure, especially canals which allowed the economical movement of raw material to their works and distribution of finished articles to their points of sale.

In the latter half of the eighteenth century, other ironmakers discovered the benefits of using coke to smelt iron, causing the production of high-quality iron to increase dramatically. In 1775, Henry Cort, a retired naval officer, purchased a small ironworks just outside the city of Plymouth in the West Country. Cort looked at ways of improving the quality of iron, and in 1784, he patented the puddling process, where melted pig iron produced using Darby's technique was combined with air and iron ore and then hammered to remove impurities. This process produced a much more malleable, less brittle wrought iron which could be passed through rollers to produce lengths of iron bar and rail. Unfortunately, Cort lost his patent when it was discovered that his business partner had financed his research using stolen money. His process for the production of wrought iron became known and widely copied, and by the end of the eighteenth century, the production of wrought iron in Britain had increased by 400%.

The use of steam engines in the smelting process made the production of iron even more economical, and the growing demand for these engines also meant an increase in demand for iron. The Napoleonic Wars were also very beneficial to the British iron industry. Demand for weapons and other items from the military boosted production, and the blockade of British ports made the import of iron from Europe virtually impossible. In the period 1793 to 1815, British production of iron quadrupled. When Napoleon was finally defeated at Waterloo in 1815, demand dropped and the price of iron fell, but this was to be only a brief setback.

By 1825, the demand for iron was being boosted by the growth of railways. Iron was needed not just to manufacture locomotives and rolling stock but also to make rails and build bridges, gantries, and signaling equipment. When demand for iron for building new railways began to drop in Great Britain, the British iron industry began to export large quantities of iron rails and other items to countries which were building their own rail systems. British iron production was around 12,000 metric tons per year in the early 1700s. By 1850, Britain was producing over two million tons of iron each year. By 1875, Great Britain was the leading producer of iron in the world with an annual output of well over six million tons each year. Iron also became popular in a whole range of other applications including being used for making things like window frames. The use of iron became so widespread that 1825 is sometimes referred to as the beginning of a new Iron Age. In 1854, a British journalist wrote: "There is no subject more important to the country than the success of the iron trade, and whatever cause may tend to affect the position to which we have once attained, it cannot but be a matter of general interest."

It would not be an exaggeration to say that, without the growth in the iron industry and the improvements in the quality of iron introduced by men like Abraham Darby and Henry Cort, the Industrial Revolution could not have happened. Iron was essential to the building of new machinery, including steam engines. The iron industry retained its importance until 1856 when a British inventor, Henry Bessemer, sparked another revolution when he came up with an economical way of converting pig iron into steel, but that is a story which does not rightfully belong in this account of the Industrial Revolution.

Chapter Three

The Power of Steam

"I sell here, Sir, what all the world desires to have—power!"

—Matthew Boulton

In the early eighteenth century, most industries in Britain were powered by human and animal muscle. Things were manufactured as quickly as people, horses, or donkeys could walk, pedal, or wind a handle. Products were transported between stages of the manufacturing process by the same means. Most production came from small businesses run by artisans and located close to the center of production of raw materials. To move industry to the next level, what was needed was motive power which could be used to operate machines of greater size and capacity.

Some mills harnessed the power of water. Built next to rivers, these mills used water to turn large paddle wheels which provided power to machinery. Some mills used wind, utilizing giant sails to catch any passing breeze. However, this meant that mills had to be built next to rivers or in areas where there was frequent wind, and they were directly affected by the weather—a long dry spell or a period of windless days could mean a lack power for the mill. What was needed was a source of power which would allow mills to be located anywhere and to be completely independent of the weather.

The first steam engine to be used in an industrial setting was the steam pump developed by English engineer and inventor Thomas Savery in 1698. The pump was extremely low-powered and inefficient by later standards, but it allowed water to be pumped out of mines to a depth of 150 feet. This allowed the exploitation of coal mines which had previously been inaccessible due to flooding, and the "Miner's Friend" was installed at several mines in the south of England.

Another English inventor, ironmonger and lay preacher Thomas Newcomen, improved on Savery's design and produced the first reliable and practical steam engine in 1712. These were very large engines which produced an impressive (for the time) five horsepower. In general, these engines were used as pumps at mines and allowed coal to be extracted at much greater depths by keeping galleries and chambers free of water. By the time that Newcomen died in 1729, about 110 of his engines were in use in Great Britain and Europe.

It took the genius of Scottish inventor, mechanical engineer, and chemist James Watt to improve the ideas of Savery and Newcomen to the point where he produced a design for a steam engine so efficient that it powered most of the Industrial Revolution. Watt was working as an instrument maker at the University of Glasgow when he was given a Newcomen steam pump to repair. It was the first time he had seen a steam engine and, he later claimed, during a Sunday afternoon walk, he devised several improvements to this device. These improvements including the use of a jacket around the boiler (to maintain temperature) and the provision of a steam condenser chamber to more efficiently control the movement of steam.

These improvements coupled with improvements in metallurgy and manufacturing tolerances meant that Watt's engines were much more efficient than those that had gone before—it took only one-quarter of the coal needed to power a Newcomen engine to power a Watt engine. However, the main advantage of the Watt engine was that it could be used not just as a pump, but to power rotating machinery, something the Savery and Newcomen engines could not easily do. Early Watt steam engines produced around ten horsepower, double the power of Newcomen engines (Watt was the first to use horsepower as a way of measuring the power of an engine).

Watt went into partnership with wealthy English manufacturer Matthew Boulton to form the company of Boulton & Watt in 1775. From its manufacturing center in Birmingham, the company marketed both a steam pump using Watt's new ideas and a double-acting rotating steam engine with a flywheel and governor which could be used to power rotating machinery in a factory or industrial works. By 1800, the company had sold more than five hundred of their steam engines, and this power source, more than any other, provided the motive power for the Industrial Revolution.

In the iron, copper, and lead industries, the availability of steam power combined with cheap coal delivered via canals led to a significant reduction in costs and improvements in quality. Previously, blast furnaces had been powered by leather bellows, often operated by humans or animals. These were replaced by cast iron blowing chambers supplied with air by a steam pump. This allowed the blast furnace to be operated at higher temperatures which helped to remove impurities in the metal. It wasn't long before steam power was also being used in other parts of the production process—steam hammers streamlined the process of the production of wrought iron even further. Due to the availability of steam power, iron production rose notably towards the end of the eighteenth century. Improvements in the quality of the metal produced led to the ability to make larger steam boilers, which made it possible to produce even more powerful steam engines, which were used to extract coal from even deeper mines and produce even better quality iron.

It didn't take long for enterprising inventors to see other uses for the steam engine. James Watt himself was one of the first people to attach a screw propeller to a steam engine. This would allow a ship to be propelled for the first time by its own motive power rather than relying on the wind. The first steam-powered ship was the *Pyroscaphe,* a small paddle-steamer built in France in 1783. The *Pyroscaphe* made its brief maiden voyage on the river Saône where the engine failed after just fifteen minutes. Other designs proved more durable, and soon steam-powered barges were being used on British canals. The development of steamships was very rapid indeed, and by 1845, the first iron-built, steam-powered transatlantic liner, the SS *Great Britain,* was regularly taking four thousand passengers to America and even to Australia.

On land, engineers were considering the use of steam to power vehicles. The snappily titled "machine à feu pour le transport de wagons et surtout de l'artillerie" ("machine powered by fire for the transport of goods and particularly artillery") was a steam-powered wagon built in France in 1769 by Nicolas-Joseph Cugnot and is generally recognized as the very first self-propelled road vehicle. Many other steam-powered wagons followed, but it was the development of steam vehicles designed to run on rails that proved most successful. Horse-drawn vehicles running on rails were in use in a number of industrial and mining centers in the late 1700s, but it wasn't until 1802 that mining engineer and inventor Richard Trevithick built the Coalbrookdale locomotive for hauling heavy loads at the Darby family's Coalbrookdale ironworks in Shropshire, England. By 1830, the very first regular goods and passenger railway operations were beginning at the Liverpool and Manchester Railway in the Midlands of England. The massive explosion of railways wouldn't happen until after the end of the Industrial Revolution, but the technology that allowed it to happen was all developed during this period.

By 1800, there were more than 1,250 steam engines in use in Great Britain, and by 1830, they were the single most common power source used in manufacturing and industry. The introduction of reliable, powerful steam engines enabled massive changes in the manufacturing of many items with production shifting from small, home-based units to large factories. This, in turn, encouraged the urbanization of this period with large numbers of people flocking to cities to take advantage of employment in factories. The steam engine produced fundamental changes comparable to the widespread introduction of the computer from the 1990s. However, in one industry in particular, the availability of steam power changed everything—the textile industry in Britain would never be the same after the introduction of Watt's double-acting engine.

Chapter Four

Mechanization of the Textile Industry

"And was Jerusalem builded here among those dark Satanic mills?"

—William Blake

Up to the middle of the eighteenth century, textile production in Great Britain was a cottage industry using mainly flax and wool. Typically, textiles were produced in the homes of weavers with the female members of the family spinning yarn and the male members using a hand-operated loom to produce the finished cloth. As a result, textiles were in short supply and relatively expensive. In the space of little more than fifty years, new technologies, inventions, and developments coupled with the availability of new raw materials completely changed the textile industry into one of the most mechanized industries in the world.

In the late 1600s and early 1700s, wool was the main raw material used for the production of textiles in Britain. Wool was produced mainly in the West Riding, the West Country, and East Anglia. These areas were close to sheep farms which produced wool and to sources of coal which were used to heat and create dyes. The wool industry was one of the oldest in England and a significant source of income for large numbers of people. Flax was used to manufacture linen and was also produced as a cottage industry. However, from the beginning of the eighteenth century, a new material began to be used to produce textiles in Britain.

Cotton was mainly grown on plantations in the southern states of America. While America was a colonial possession of Britain, large quantities of raw cotton were imported, but there were problems with creating cotton cloth. First of all, cotton can be most easily woven in a damp climate, and the existing wool producing areas in the south-east were simply too dry. Instead, cotton was largely processed in the damper conditions of Lancashire and Glasgow. There were also problems in weaving the new material—the light cotton thread was not strong enough to be used to create the warp in hand-operated looms and often had to be combined with a wool or linen warp to produce materials such as fustian. Despite this, cotton cloth was a revelation in early eighteenth-century Britain—it was relatively light, comfortable to wear, and could easily be printed with bright, colorful designs. By 1721, the popularity of cotton fabric was so great that the British Parliament passed an act banning the wearing of printed fabrics. This was done because of concerns that the production of cotton and cotton cloth was a threat to the wool industry.

Production of cotton cloth continued even after the act (which applied only to printed cloth), but there was a major problem—spinning cotton thread was much slower than spinning wool, and in the home-based production still largely used, the production of thread often lagged far behind the capacity of weaving looms. It wasn't until Lancashire weaver and inventor James Hargreaves invented the Spinning Jenny ("Jenny" was a colloquial term for any form of machine at the time) that it was suddenly possible to produce sufficient thread to keep up with weaving. In 1769, businessman and inventor Richard Arkwright patented the water frame, a mechanized device which combined Hargreaves' invention with a water-powered machine which could produce vast quantities of much stronger cotton thread. For the first time, cotton could be used for both the warp and the weave of cloth, and lightweight cotton fabrics became possible.

However, the production of cotton thread using Arkwright's methods required large machines and an adjacent supply of running water. For the first time, the production of thread was done in large factories, though weaving was still generally done in a network of home-based producers. Recognizing the growing significance of the cotton industry in Britain, in 1774 the government repealed the 1721 act banning printed fabrics. Demand for cotton grew exponentially, and producers looked at ways to mechanize the process even further.

With the automation of the spinning of cotton thread, supply was able not just to keep pace with demand from weavers but to produce more thread than they could possibly use. Then, in 1784, the invention by Edmund Cartwright of the power loom mechanized the weaving of cotton and suddenly what had been a cottage industry exploded into one of the most mechanized industries in the world. Within little more than fifty years, there were more than one-quarter of a million power looms in Great Britain. These were beyond the capacity of a single family to own and operate, and for the first time, cotton production was centered in factories where large numbers of people could congregate to produce cotton cloth.

Initially, power looms relied on water wheels to provide energy. Before long, it became apparent that the steam engine produced by Boulton & Watt could be used to provide a more reliable, efficient, and consistent source of power. However, the initial investment required to build a weaving works powered by steam engines was very large, and to recoup that investment it made sense to make these as large as possible. This idea also relied on the improved transport infrastructure, and especially the new network of canals to bring raw material to these large factories and to distribute the finished product.

This type of mechanization brought fundamental changes. Instead of being spread out across a myriad of small producers in rural areas, the spinning of cotton thread and the weaving of cotton fabric became concentrated in a small number of large factories. These factories needed large numbers of workers; some factory operators built towns and villages just to accommodate their workers. For the first time, a new manufacturing process actually created new urban centers. The mechanization and concentration of cotton manufacturing led to an explosion in production, a fall in costs, and a plentiful supply of the popular new fabrics.

In the early 1700s, Britain imported around two million pounds of cotton annually. By 1790, Britain was importing more than thirty million pounds of raw cotton each year, mainly from America and India. In 1800, Britain imported almost sixty million pounds of raw cotton. By the end of the eighteenth century, cotton production accounted for 5% of Britain's total national income. By 1812, there were one hundred thousand people involved in the cotton spinning industry in Britain and more than one-quarter of a million involved in weaving. By this time, cotton production accounted for more than 8% of the national income and had overtaken wool. By 1830, the export of cotton textiles accounted for more than half of Britain's total exports and the cotton industry accounted for more than 30% of the total working population of the country.

The growth of the cotton industry also brought major demographic changes to Britain. In 1760, Manchester was a small town with a population of around 17,000 people.

Sixty years later, Manchester was at the center of British cotton production and had a population of more than 180,000. The port of Liverpool, the main port for Manchester, grew at a similar rate. By 1850, an area within a radius of 50 miles from Manchester accounted for more than 40% of the total worldwide production of cotton textiles. Britain's production of cotton was so efficient that countries such as America were forced to impose heavy tariffs on imported British cotton to prevent still mainly hand-produced American cotton from being forced out of business completely. Textile production was so important to the British economy that a new act was passed making it illegal to export textile machinery or designs.

Not only did these new urban centers draw in large numbers of people who had previously lived in rural areas, but they also shifted the balance of power in Great Britain. As towns in the new industrial areas of the Midlands grew, towns such as Norwich in East Anglia which had previously been at the center of the wool industry declined in terms of population and importance. Even London, traditionally the center of power in Britain, began to feel the competition from the new areas.

The cotton industry provided work for large numbers of people in Great Britain at a time when the population was increasing rapidly. In some ways this was beneficial—without the cotton industry, unemployment would have been a major issue. However, the new factories needed mainly unskilled workers who were paid low wages, and this created a new phenomenon—large urban areas populated by people who lived only a few short steps from poverty, even though they were employed.

Chapter Five

The Lives of Workers during the Industrial Revolution

"The process of industrialization is necessarily painful. It must involve the erosion of traditional patterns of life. But it was carried through with exceptional violence in Britain."

—E.P. Thompson, The Making of the English Working Class

The textile industry provides a useful snapshot of the changes in working practices which accompanied the Industrial Revolution. In the early part of the eighteenth century, textiles were produced by an extensive network of home-based workers. Whole families were involved in working in their own homes (though as few as three people could run a spinning or weaving business), and even children were taught at an early age to help in the family business. Many of these businesses were based in small villages or towns, and most supplemented their earnings by keeping a garden in which to grow vegetables or even in which to nurture a few livestock. Hours and holidays were set by the family, and the small-scale, hand-operated machinery presented little danger of injury for any of the workers. The intensity of work could be varied to suit the rhythms of the countryside, and the family was able to spend a great deal of time together.

But existence wasn't always bucolic for home-based spinners and weavers. There was no readily accessible healthcare, and sickness or illness for one member of the family might mean that it wasn't possible to continue production. The supply of raw materials could be impacted by the weather and other factors as could the distribution of finished cloth. These things affected income and, as there wasn't any form of assistance available from local authorities, a lack of income could mean a lack of food on the table.

In the factories which grew during this period, life was very different. In 1771, Richard Arkwright, inventor of the water frame, began building what is now recognized as one of the first factories ever created. Cromford Mill in Derbyshire was built specifically to produce spun cotton using Arkwright's water frame. The five-story building was constructed on the bank of the River Derwent, a small river which drew some of its water from drainings from the nearby Wirksworth lead mines. This ensured a year-round supply of water (the water drained from the mine was warm which ensured that the river did not freeze in winter) that was used to power the machinery in the mill. The mill opened in 1772, and from the outset it ran day and night with workers divided into two, twelve-hour shifts.

Initially, the factory employed 200 people, but within 15 years it had expanded to require 800 workers. This was well beyond the capacity of the sparsely populated local area, so Arkwright built housing, a church, and a school for his workers. Apart from engineers who were required to ensure that the machinery kept running smoothly, most employees at Cromford Mill were unskilled—the machinery did the actual spinning of the thread, and all workers had to do was ensure that it kept running and was supplied with raw materials. Arkwright was an astute businessman, and he quickly realized that he could maximize profits by employing mainly women and children as unskilled workers (then, as now, women were generally paid less than men). Two-thirds of the workers employed by Arkwright were children, and he refused to employ anyone over the age of forty. He preferred to have weaving families living in the cottages close to the mill because while the women and children of the family would work at the mill, the man would stay at home and weave with the cotton thread produced at the mill.

Children as young as seven were employed in the mill. Children were popular as employees because they were cheaper than women and they were small enough to be able to squeeze into small spaces between machines. Their small hands were useful for tying-up broken threads in hard-to-reach areas. There was also a ready supply of child workers—overcrowded orphanages could quickly replace those injured or killed. Arkwright was generally considered to be a caring employer—for example, he insisted that his child workers received at least a basic education while employed. However, by modern standards, Cromford Mill was a dangerous and oppressive place to work. There was no sick pay, and workers often dragged themselves into work while ill (and often spread the illness to their colleagues) rather than risk losing pay. Workers could be fined for a whole range of infarctions including whistling and looking out of the window.

Arkwright was obsessive about punctuality; the only gate to the factory was closed and locked promptly at six in the morning and six in the evening, the times at which the day and night shifts started. Any worker who arrived after the gates had closed was not allowed to enter and would lose a day's pay. As a further incentive, they would also be fined the equivalent of one additional day's pay. Being absent from work without permission resulted in even more draconian penalties. The *Derby Mercury* newspaper carried the following piece about one of Arkwright's employees in November 1777: "John Jefferies, a gunsmith of Cromford, has been committed to the House of Correction at Derby for one month; and to be kept to hard labour. John Jefferies was charged by Mr. Arkwright, Cotton Merchant, with having absented himself from his master's business without leave."

A desire to be absent wasn't surprising given that conditions inside the factory were far from pleasant. The constantly running machinery produced a deafening cacophony of noise, and there was no form of ear protection available. None of the machinery had any form of safety guards, making it horribly easy for workers to become entangled and dragged in. None of the workers had any form of safety clothing, and the loose-fitting clothing of the day was very prone to being caught in machinery. Children were particularly at risk. In addition to working as piecers (tying broken threads while the machinery continued to operate), small children were also popular as scavengers, which entailed picking up loose cotton from underneath running machinery. One man who worked as a scavenger at Arkwright's mill later recalled: "The scavenger has to take the brush and sweep under the wheels, and to be under the direction of the spinners and the piecers generally. I frequently had to be under the wheels, and in consequence of the perpetual motion of the machinery, I was liable to accidents constantly. I was very frequently obliged to lie flat, to avoid being run over or caught."

Young children were expected to work the same twelve-hour shifts as adults, and it has been calculated that the average shift involved walking more than twenty miles in addition to other physical work. Exhaustion and fatigue added to the risk of injury or death. In addition to the risk from machinery, in parts of the mill, especially the carding room, the air was thick with cotton dust. Breathing this dust for extended periods produced acute and debilitating lung conditions which afflicted many workers. A man named John Reed later told a committee investigating conditions in factories how he had first been employed as a child worker in Cromford Mill at the age of nine. By the age of 19, he was so crippled by a combination of injuries and a lung condition that he was unable to continue working. He was dismissed without any form of pension or compensation and forced to subsist as best he could.

It's worth remembering that Cromford Mill was, at the time, regarded as an enlightened place of work and Arkwright as a considerate employer. Other businessmen were less scrupulous, and when it became apparent that Cromford Mill was very profitable and Arkwright wealthy, many other entrepreneurs became interested in building similar factories. Many were keen to maximize potential profits even if that placed workers at more risk. Arkwright himself went on to build new factories in Lancashire, Staffordshire, and at New Lanark in Scotland. Most of these factories were similar in design to Cromford Mills, though they were intended to use steam engines for motive power rather than a water mill, with steam pipes and hot engines making conditions even more hazardous for workers.

Arkwright became very wealthy indeed. He bought a stately home close to the mill and then a castle on a nearby hill, Willersley Manor. Arkwright was made high sheriff of Derbyshire, and in 1786, he was knighted by King George III. Arkwright died in 1792 at the age of 59. He left a fortune worth £500,000 (over £200 million in current value). Factories like those he had built at Cromford and New Lanark became commonplace. By 1800, there were

900 cotton mills in Great Britain. By 1830, the average cotton mill in Manchester employed more than 400 people. The day of the home spinning and weaving industry were long gone, swamped in a tidal wave of more efficient and profitable factories and mills.

The rise of factories also brought about fundamental changes in British society. Instead of being spread across the country, people began to congregate in urban centers where there were factories and work. Completely new urban centers developed around clusters of factories and mills. At the same time, the numbers of skilled workers declined. For example, the invention of the power loom meant that weaving could be done by unskilled machine operators. By 1830, there were fifty thousand of these machines operating in Britain and the occupation of weaver had essentially disappeared, replaced by poorly paid unskilled workers.

The first effective act of Parliament which sought to improve conditions for workers in factories was the Cotton Mills and Factories Act of 1819. The act made it illegal to employ children under nine years of age and made the maximum length of the working day twelve hours for children of up to sixteen years old. The fact that this was seen both as enlightened and a major step forward in the protection of child workers tells us a great deal about just how dreadful conditions in British factories must have been.

In contrast, the middle class in Great Britain, the shopkeepers, teachers, accountants, and clerks whose jobs could not be replaced by machinery, prospered. Shops, for example, could be located close to urban centers and be assured of a continuing supply of prospective customers. Accountants and clerks were kept in work by the growing needs of factories. These middle-class families not only had disposable income, they were able to spend it on the cheap, mass-produced products of the factories such as furniture and clothes.

The rise of factories and mass production was an essential element of the Industrial Revolution, and it brought great wealth for a very small number of people and a moderate improvement for the small but growing middle class. However, for the mass of ordinary people condemned to unskilled, poorly paid, and dangerous work, it meant unremitting poverty and hardship. While Richard Arkwright was able to amass a personal fortune worth half a million pounds in the space of just twenty years, many of his workers were paid four pence a day, a subsistence wage that gave no opportunity to accrue savings. The dangers of the workplace were combined with a lack of sick pay or compensation for injury and illness and a complete lack of any form of pension. In 2007, British economist Professor Gregory Clark calculated that the average working family in Britain in 1800 were no better off in material terms than the primitive hunter-gatherers who had lived in the same area one hundred thousand years before.

In these circumstances, it is unsurprising that the Industrial Revolution also led directly to the establishment of social movements which would support the rights of workers and help to shape and define the nineteenth and twentieth centuries.

Chapter Six

The Rise of Labor Movements

"I have been in some of the most oppressed provinces of Turkey; but never, under the most despotic of infidel governments, did I behold such squalid wretchedness as I have seen since my return, in the very heart of a Christian country."

—Lord Byron

On February 27, 1812, a newly appointed 24-year-old lord stood up in the House of Lords to make his maiden speech. It wasn't a commonplace speech (the quote above is an extract), but then George Gordon Byron, popular poet and romantic hero, wasn't a commonplace lord. The purpose of Byron's first speech as a lord was to oppose the Frame Work Bill, a proposed act of Parliament which sought to make the deliberate damage of factory machinery or equipment a capital offense punishable by death. This speech neatly encapsulates the two different but linked strands of opposition to the rise of factories and mechanization—the Luddites were skilled workers who saw their livelihoods threatened by the new technology and responded with violence while the Romantics were intellectuals who yearned for a return to a simpler, more rural and agrarian form of life in Britain.

In his speech, Lord Byron referred to the practice of many of the wealthy classes who referred to those who opposed the rise of industrialization as "the mob." He said: "It is the mob that labor in your fields and serve in your houses, that man your navy and recruit your army, that have enabled you to defy all the world, and can also defy you when neglect and calamity have driven them to despair. You may well call the people a mob, but do not forget that a mob often speaks the sentiments of the people."

Despite Byron's impassioned speech, the Frame Work Bill passed into law and being found guilty of destroying factory machinery became punishable by hanging. Just what had happened to make Parliament so terrified of the destruction of factories and their machinery that they would introduce a law of such severity?

In the early 1800s, a new word entered the vocabulary of the English language: Luddite. The term referred to groups of people who were opposed to the mechanization of previously skilled work in the textile industry including spinning and weaving. The name comes from a fictitious character, Ned Ludd, an apprentice who was said to have smashed two mechanical knitting machines. Ludd, like Robin Hood, then went to hide-out in Sherwood Forest where he was promoted to King Ludd or General Ludd and encouraged bands of disaffected workers to smash the machines that were taking their jobs. There never was a real Ned Ludd, but his name and the term Luddite became used for everyone who opposed the rise of industrialization (and is still used today as a derogatory term for anyone who opposes technology of any kind).

The movement of opposition to mechanization really started in the north of England in the 1780s when isolated groups of workers attempted to destroy automated spinning and weaving machinery. These events prompted the passing of the Protection of Stocking Frames, etc. Act in 1788, which made the deliberate destruction of such equipment punishable by transportation for up to 14 years. Penal transportation entailed being sent off to a colony to serve the sentence.

The destruction of machinery remained rare, and it wasn't until 1811 that larger bands of Luddites attacked factories in Nottinghamshire, Lancashire, and Yorkshire. It wasn't an organized, national movement, even though wealthy industrialists saw it as such; it was mainly made up of small, isolated groups of skilled workers who were either unemployed or feared that they soon would be. These groups met in secret and planned attacks on prominent factories and mills. Some factory owners became so concerned that they had secret chambers built inside their factories where they could hide in safety if the Luddites attacked—a precursor to today's safe rooms. Their fears weren't completely unfounded—Yorkshire mill owner William Horsfall (a man who had promised that he would "ride up to his saddle in Luddite blood") was assassinated by Luddites in April 1812.

Some of the Luddite attacks on factories were large-scale affairs. On April 20, 1812, a group of around three thousand Luddites looted shops in the town of Middleton in Lancashire, around five miles from the city of Manchester. They then mounted an attack on the mill of Daniel Burton & Sons which was provided with steam-powered spinning looms. Armed workers inside the mill opened fire; at least five Luddites were shot dead and many more were injured. It wasn't until the arrival of units of the British army that the Luddites were finally repulsed. The following day, after a night of rioting and the burning of some houses, the Luddites clashed once again with cavalry and infantry units of the British army. Around twelve Luddites were killed and around one hundred wounded. The army expended around two thousand rounds of ammunition during the conflict.

In the months that followed, there were a number of clashes between units of the army and Luddite protestors. During this period, the height of Britain's involvement in the Napoleonic Wars, more British soldiers were involved in fighting the Luddites than were fighting the French. These weren't isolated protests—the desperation of unemployed workers was driving something very close to a full-scale insurrection in some parts of northern England.

The government's response was prompt and brutal. Around seventy Luddites were hanged, and hundreds more were transported for life or shorter periods. In 1817, an armed uprising by around three hundred unemployed weavers and spinners in the village of Pentrich in Derbyshire, which was crushed by constabulary armed by mill owners and elements of the British army, marked the effective end of the Luddite movement. However, the Luddites weren't the only group to be opposed to the industrialization of Great Britain.

Lord Byron was one of the first examples of the celebrity social activist, but he wasn't the only activist in early nineteenth-century Britain. Byron was just one of a loose group of influential poets who became known as the Romantics. Poetry was wildly popular in the early 1800s—when Byron's epic poem *Childe Harold* was published in 1812, the first edition sold out within three days, and Byron became, virtually overnight, a national and international celebrity. In addition to Byron, poets including William Wordsworth, Samuel Taylor Coleridge, William Blake, and Percy Bysshe Shelley were producing poems that were not just popular but also politically radical. Shelley, for example, in addition to poetry, wrote an essay entitled *A Philosophical View of Reform* which was considered so incendiary that it was suppressed in Britain for over one hundred years.

Byron, Shelley, and other Romantic poets produced works which looked back at a supposedly utopian rural past in England and deplored the spread of factories and giant mills. Other writers and artists took up the same message. Shelley's wife, Mary Wollstonecraft Shelley, wrote a best-selling Gothic horror novel, *Frankenstein*, which can be read as a warning against reliance on science and technology, and the artist John Constable produced a range of paintings showing a highly romanticized version of English rural life and landscape.

The Romantics were influential in inspiring a longing for a previous, simpler life, even if their version of that life ignored the inconvenient fact that life was just as brutally short for agricultural workers in the seventeenth century as it was for factory workers in the eighteenth. Nevertheless, neither the violence of the Luddites nor the longing of the Romantics could turn back the tide. The mass of people may have agreed to some extent with both groups, but they also wanted access to the cheap, mass-produced goods which were produced by factories, and they needed the work these new industrial centers provided. The host of inventions and developments which enabled the Industrial Revolution could not be undone. Urbanization and the need for unskilled labor continued to grow in Britain and the other countries to which the Industrial Revolution spread.

The Industrial Revolution also marked the beginning of other movements which were not dedicated to turning back the clock but to helping workers live and thrive in the new industrial landscape. In the period following the end of the Napoleonic Wars in 1815, Great Britain experienced a period of high unemployment as thousands of soldiers were discharged from the army and needed work. This was combined with famine exacerbated by the Corn Laws, tariffs placed on imported food and grain to protect domestic producers. The laws helped farmers, but it also increased the price of basic foodstuffs and meant hunger and hardship for the increasing numbers of working-class people surviving on low wages.

Although Great Britain was nominally a democracy during the Industrial Revolution, the truth was that only small numbers of people were allowed to vote. A survey in 1780 found that less than 3% of the total population had the right to vote, and new industrial cities such as Manchester and Birmingham had no members of Parliament at all. This situation led to a rise in political movements calling for electoral reform. These activists were quite different from the Romantics and the Luddites—they had no issue with technological progress nor industrialization, they simply wanted a more equable division of the profits.

One such movement was the Manchester Patriotic Union, a popular electoral group centered in the city of Manchester and drawing much of its membership from unskilled workers in factories and mills. On August 16, 1819, this group organized a demonstration at St Peter's Field, a piece of open ground on the outskirts of Manchester. No-one is quite sure how many people attended the meeting, estimates vary from 60,000 to 150,000, but it was certainly one of the largest public demonstrations that had ever been seen in Britain. Though the meeting was planned in advance and perfectly legal, the response of the authorities was heavy-handed and brutal. Members of the Yeomanry, a local militia, attempted to force their way into the crowd to arrest the speakers. This resulted in the deaths of a child and a woman. In response, the crowd surrounded a small group of soldiers. Alarmed, the local magistrate called in the 15th Hussars. This elite cavalry unit charged into the mass of unarmed protestors with sabers drawn. Fifteen people were killed on the spot, and around seven hundred were injured, some gravely.

Many journalists from British newspapers were present, and the massacre was widely reported. It became known as the Peterloo Massacre, an ironic reference to the Battle of Waterloo which had taken place just four years earlier. An unemployed weaver who had been a soldier at Waterloo was one of those injured at Peterloo. He died of his wounds a few days later, but before his death he told a journalist: "At Waterloo there was man to man but there it was downright murder."

Most ordinary people were horrified and outraged at the massacre. Yet those involved in organizing and speaking at the protest were arrested and brought to court. Many were jailed, some were transported. Some of the families of those killed tried to take the Yeomanry and the 15th Hussars to court, but these cases were all thrown out. New laws were introduced to reduce the right to protest, and by 1820, every working-class political radical calling for Parliamentary reform was in prison. One modern historian has compared the plight of working-class people in the north of England in the early years of the nineteenth century with that of blacks in twentieth-century South Africa.

The desire for change and reform amongst the new working class created by the Industrial Revolution could not be denied indefinitely. The Great Reform Act of 1832 was just the first act of Parliament to extend suffrage and to ensure that the new industrial cities had their own members of Parliament—amongst other things, the new act gave 22 cities two MPs each.

When Karl Marx moved to Britain in 1850 and began work on what would become *Das Kapital*, the book which would ultimately lead to the formation of Communism as a political movement, he was influenced and inspired by the workers' struggle for electoral reform which had arisen from the Industrial Revolution. Although the Industrial

Revolution may not have been a revolution in the conventional sense, it transformed Britain's society and Parliament completely.

Conclusion

No one invention or development made the Industrial Revolution possible. Instead, a number of relatively small changes interacted, often in unforeseen ways, to produce change that was sudden and complete. Abraham Darby's improvements in iron smelting produced better quality iron which enabled the manufacture of more effective and reliable steam engines, which in turn enabled more efficient ways of producing iron. Steam engines and better quality iron enabled the creation of automated machines for weaving and spinning which led to large-scale mills and factories. Canals and improvements in roads allowed these factories to import raw materials and distribute finished products. All these things happened first in Great Britain and, combined with the ready availability of iron ore and coal, this made England the most technologically advanced country in the world. These changes also gradually spread to other countries, but it was in Great Britain that the changes had the most impact.

By 1850, Great Britain (not including its many colonial possessions) had become the first, modern, industrialized nation and accounted for 10% of the GDP of the entire world. The British Empire was the most powerful empire in the world and included Canada, Australia, New Zealand, India, the West Indies, Hong Kong, and large parts of Africa. Great Britain had the most powerful navy in the world, and the British army, though tiny in size, would win wars in China, Russia, and India virtually simultaneously in the 1850s. Britain was known as "the Workshop of the World," and British shipbuilding and industry were the most advanced in the world. All these things were directly attributable to the Industrial Revolution.

Of course, not all aspects of the Industrial Revolution were beneficial. Rapid industrialization led to equally rapid urbanization, and large numbers of people found themselves working in exhausting and dangerous conditions for low pay and living in poor quality housing. Much of the urban squalor which has become associated with the Victorian period originated in the Industrial Revolution. The Luddites who tried to oppose the growth of automation and industrialization were ruthlessly and sometimes brutally crushed, as were those who first campaigned for Parliamentary and electoral reform. The authorities seemed to make little distinction between violent Luddites and peaceful protestors—anyone who stood in the way of progress was regarded as a dangerous reactionary and treated as such.

Nothing in the developed world would ever be quite the same after the Industrial Revolution. People became used to working in disciplined, large-scale environments and living in mass housing close to their place of work. People also became used to cheap, mass-produced clothes, furniture, and other items—the Industrial Revolution can be seen as the beginning of the modern consumer society. Other issues which are familiar to us today such as technophobia, distrust of large companies, concerns about global trade, and the effects of industry on the environment can also be traced back to the Industrial Revolution. This is one revolution which continues to have an impact on almost every aspect of today's world.

Printed in Great Britain
by Amazon